Just COCKTAILS

A BARTENDER'S GUIDE

Compiled *and* Edited *by*
W. C. WHITFIELD

DECORATIONS BY TAD SHELL

VANCOUVER:
ENGAGE BOOKS LIMITED
2013

e

Engage Books
Mailing address
PO BOX 4608
Main Station Terminal
349 West Georgia Street
Vancouver, BC
Canada, V6B 4A1

www.engagebooks.ca

Edited by: Tad Shell
Illustrated by: Tad Shell
Designed by: A.R. Roumanis

ISBN: 978-1-927970-01-0

FIRST EDITION / FIRST PRINTING

Contents

Then to the Flowing Bowl
        did I adjourn
My lips the Secret Well
        of Life to learn,
And lip to lip it murmur'd -
        "While you live,
Drink! -for once dead you
        never shall return"

-OMAR KHAYYAM

A Real American Institution

We of this new world known as the United States of America are prone to yield the palm of cookery to the old world on the other side of the Atlantic.

As witness of this point take note of the fact that the famous chefs of our grandest hotels are almost invariably French, or Italian, or Spanish—usually of Latin origin, anyway. And every historic restaurant of gay New York and old New Orleans, almost without exception, gained its "place in the sun" because of the culinary skill of a foreigner.

But when it comes to the art of mixing drinks—well, that is a "horse of another color". In that field the new world tops the old—and how! The American bartender of the "Gay Nineties" was an institution. His fame spread to the four corners of the globe, and visitors to our shores from the continent bowed before his skill in concocting tempting mixtures of "liquid lightning". He was—and still is—in a class by himself. We may go to Europe for our chefs, but Europe comes to us for its bartenders.

Just why the American excels in this field is hard to say, but it is possibly for the same reason that we lead the world in inventive genius (an acknowledged fact). That reason is that we will "try anything once". We are not so tied by age-old conventions, are not so content to let custom rule us. We like to experiment in all fields, and so—when it comes to mixing drinks—we stop at nothing.

It is possible, of course, that many digestive tracts have been impaired by these experiments (we will concede that much to the abstainers), but the discovery that a smooth, mellow Manhattan cocktail will work miracles with a laggard appetite certainly makes up for such damages. And the soothing qualities of Creme de Cacao blended with "Cream de Cow" has done such wonders for those same digestive tracts that we can surely forgive some mistakes.

So here's to the Knight of the Brass Rail, and his many good deeds —quiet a few of which you will find on the following pages:—

MEASUREMENTS

1 DASH	1/3 TEASPOON
1 BARSPOON	1/2 TEASPOON
1 TEASPOON	1/3 TABLESPOON
1 TABLESPOON	1/2 FLUID OUNCE
1 PONY	1 FLUID OUNCE
1 JIGGER	1½ FLUID OUNCES
1 WINEGLASS	2 FLUID OUNCES

THE JIGGER ORIGINALLY HELD TWO OUNCES, BUT THAT WAS BEFORE PROHIBITION. IT HAS SINCE SHRUNK TO 1½ OUNCES.

THE USE OF A SHAKER IN MIXING COCKTAILS MEANS FAST MELTING ICE, AND A WEAKER, THINNER DRINK. IF YOU WANT POTENCY USE A MIXING GLASS AND A SPOON.

SUGAR IS NOT READILY SOLUBLE IN ALCOHOL, SO IT IS WELL TO KEEP ON HAND A SMALL AMOUNT OF SYRUP FOR SWEETENING DRINKS. THIS CAN BE MADE EASILY BY BOILING ONE POUND OF SUGAR IN ONE PINT OF WATER, AND CAN BE KEPT IN A BOTTLE.

COCKTAILS SHOULD BE SERVED IN CHILLED GLASSES. LET THEM STAND FILLED WITH SHAVED ICE WHILE THE DRINKS ARE BEING MIXED.

EQUIPMENT

STRAINER
MIXING GLASS
COCKTAIL SHAKER
LEMON SQUEEZER
LIME SQUEEZER
BARSPOON, LONG HANDLED
CORKSCREW WITH LONG SHANK
DASHER TOP, FOR BITTERS BOTTLES.
METAL JIGGER MEASURE
ICE BAG AND MALLET
WOODEN PESTLE

COCK TALES & COCKTAILS

The tale, or perhaps we should say the tales, of the cocktail, all go to prove that it is the most American of all mixed drinks.

Whether we take as our authority the story of the barmaid at the revolutionary tavern who tossed together a drink for some of Lafayette's officers, and as an afterthought snatched some feathers from a nearby rooster with which to spear the cherries, or whether we pin our faith to the legend of the buccaneers of the Spanish Main who stirred their concoctions of liquors looted from captured galleons with the plumage of West Indian Cocks, the important point is still this—the cocktail is All American, both in origin and name.

Their specific names are legion. There are more different kinds than any collection could ever contain. The most popular ones, those that are served at all bars, both private and public, number something like a score.

We have attempted to list these in the following group:—

JUST
Cocktails

OLD FASHIONED

1 JIGGER BOURBON
2 DASHES ANGOSTURA BITTERS
1/2 LUMP SUGAR
2 SPOONS WATER
STIR AND THEN ADD LUMP OF
ICE AND PIECES OF LEMON AND
ORANGE.

OLD FASHIONED
(No. 2)

1 JIGGER RYE
1 DASH ANGOSTURA BITTERS
2 DASHES ORANGE BITTERS
1 LUMP SUGAR (CRUSHED)
1 LUMP OF ICE
DECORATE WITH LEMON AND
ORANGE.

MANHATTAN

1/2 RYE WHISKEY
1/2 ITALIAN VERMOUTH
1 DASH ORANGE BITTERS
SERVE WITH A MARASCHINO
CHERRY.

MANHATTAN
(No. 2)

2/3 BOURBON
1/3 ITALIAN VERMOUTH
ADD A DASH OF ANGOSTURA
BITTERS AND A CHERRY.

GIN

1 JIGGER DRY GIN
3 DASHES BITTERS
1 TWIST LEMON PEEL

GIN (NO. 2)

1 JIGGER GIN
3 DASHES GUM SYRUP
2 DASHES ANGOSTURA BITTERS
2 DASHES CURACAO
1 TWIST LEMON PEEL

MARTINI

1/2 TOM GIN
1/2 ITALIAN VERMOUTH
1 DASH ORANGE BITTERS
SERVE WITH A GREEN OLIVE.

FRENCH MARTINI

5/6 GIN
1/6 FRENCH VERMOUTH
TWIST OF LEMON PEEL ON TOP,
SERVE WITH A GREEN OLIVE.

DRY MARTINI

2/3 GIN
1/3 FRENCH VERMOUTH
1 DASH BITTERS
TWIST OF LEMON PEEL ON TOP,
SERVE WITH A GREEN OLIVE.

PRESIDENTE
NEW ORLEANS

1 PONY RUM
1 PONY CURACAO
1 PONY FRENCH VERMOUTH
2 DASHES GRENADINE
SERVE WITH CHERRY AND
ORANGE PEEL.

PRESIDENTE
CUBAN

1 JIGGER RUM
1 LIME (JUICE ONLY)
2 DASHES GRENADINE

ALEXANDER

1 PONY GIN
1 PONY CREME DE CACAO
1 PONY FRESH CREAM

ALEXANDER'S
SPECIAL

1 PONY GIN
1 PONY CREME DE CACAO
1/2 LIME (JUICE ONLY)
1 DASH FRESH CREAM

MILLIONAIRE

1/3 JAMAICA RUM
1/3 APRICOT BRANDY
1/3 SLOE GIN
1 LIME (JUICE ONLY)
1 DASH GRENADINE

MILLIONAIRE (NO. 2)

2/3 DRY GIN
1/3 ABSINTHE (OR PERNOD)
1 WHITE OF EGG
1 DASH ANISETTE

BRANDY

1 JIGGER BEST BRANDY
2 DASHES BITTERS
1 DASH ITALIAN VERMOUTH
1 TWIST OF LEMON PEEL

DUBONNET

1/2 DUBONNET
1/2 DRY GIN

COGNAC

1/3 COGNAC
1/3 COINTREAU
1/3 LEMON JUICE

CHAMPAGNE

1/3 GLASS CRACKED ICE
1 LUMP SUGAR
2 DASHES ANGOSTURA BITTERS
1 SLICE ORANGE
CHAMPAGNE TO FILL THE FIVE
OUNCE CHAMPAGNE GOBLET WHICH
SHOULD BE USED. STIR GENTLY.

Dixie Whiskey

1 JIGGER WHISKEY
1 DASH ANGOSTURA BITTERS
2 DASHES CURACAO
4 DASHES CREME DE MENTHE
1/2 LUMP SUGAR

Whiskey

1 JIGGER WHISKEY
4 DASHES SYRUP
1 DASH BITTERS

Whiskey Sour

1/2 RYE
1/2 LEMON JUICE
POWDERED SUGAR

Sloe Gin

2/3 SLOE GIN
1/3 PLYMOUTH GIN
1 DASH ORANGE BITTERS

Bronx

1 JIGGER DRY GIN
1/2 JIGGER FRENCH VERMOUTH
1/2 JIGGER ITALIAN VERMOUTH
ADD JUICE OF 1/4 ORANGE AND
SHAKE WELL. SERVE WITH SLICE
OF ORANGE.

Bronx Express

1/3 GIN
1/3 FRENCH VERMOUTH
1/3 ORANGE JUICE
1 DASH ABSINTHE

Vermouth

1 JIGGER FRENCH VERMOUTH
1 DASH ABSINTHE
1 DASH MARASCHINO
2 DASHES BITTERS
SERVE WITH A CHERRY

Bacardi

1 JIGGER BACARDI RUM
1/2 LIME (JUICE ONLY)
2 DASHES GRENADINE

Absinthe

1 PONY ABSINTHE
1 PONY WATER
2 DASHES BITTERS
3 DASHES BENEDICTINE

Fancy Brandy

1 JIGGER FINE BRANDY
2 DASHES CURACAO
2 DASHES ANGOSTURA BITTERS
3 DASHES GUM SYRUP

—AND THEN THERE ARE

"PRETTY" COCKTAILS

Besides the group of cocktails listed in the preceding pages as the most popular (remember that you have a perfect right to disagree with this), there were quite a few in the old days that had the "call" with the fair sex, probably because the use of syrups of delicate color lent to most of them an aesthetic charm.

Of course, in this day of post-prohibition, the women-folk often pre-empt all the space at the bar, and take their liquor just as raw as the male of the species, so the pretty cocktails of the "Gay Nineties" are no longer classed as feminine in their appeal. Today they are favored by the man who likes his pre-dinner drink to have a sweeter tang to it, and perhaps not so much kick. Those who prefer to have the "hard liquor" taste disguised by fruit juices and syrups also favor this type of cocktail.

Some of the best known ones of both yesterday, meaning pre-prohibition times, and today, are given here:—

Pink Whiskers

1 PONY BRANDY
1 PONY FRENCH VERMOUTH
1/4 ORANGE (JUICE ONLY)
3 DASHES GRENADINE
1 DASH CREME DE MENTHE

Orange Blossom

1/3 TOM GIN
1/3 ITALIAN VERMOUTH
1/3 ORANGE JUICE

Paradise

1/3 GIN
1/3 APRICOT BRANDY
1/3 ORANGE JUICE

Coffee

2/3 PORT WINE
1/3 BRANDY
1 YOLK OF EGG
1 SPOON SUGAR

Creole

1/2 JIGGER BOURBON
1/2 JIGGER ITALIAN VERMOUTH
1 DASH BENEDICTINE
1 DASH MARASCHINO
1 TWIST LEMON PEEL

Magnolia Blossom

1/2 DRY GIN
1/4 FRESH CREAM
1/4 LEMON JUICE
1 DASH GRENADINE

White Rose

1 JIGGER DRY GIN
1/4 ORANGE (JUICE ONLY)
1 LIME (JUICE ONLY)
1/2 JIGGER MARASCHINO
1 WHITE OF EGG

Silver King

1 JIGGER DRY GIN
1/2 LEMON (JUICE ONLY)
1 WHITE OF EGG
2 DASHES SYRUP
2 DASHES ORANGE BITTERS

Bachelor's Bait

1 JIGGER DRY GIN
1 WHITE OF EGG
3 DASHES ORANGE BITTERS
3 DASHES GRENADINE

White Cargo

1 JIGGER DRY GIN
1 JIGGER VANILLA ICE CREAM
2 TEASPOONS WHITE WINE
SHAKE TILL THE ICE CREAM
   MELTS. NO ICE.

American Beauty

1/4 Brandy
1/4 French Vermouth
1/4 Orange Juice
1/4 Grenadine
1 dash Creme de Menthe
Top with a little Port Wine

Around the World

1/2 Pineapple Juice
1/4 Green Creme de Menthe
1/4 Dry Gin

Cafe de Paris

1 jigger Dry Gin
3 dashes Absinthe
1 teaspoon fresh cream
1 white of egg

Five Fifteen

1 pony Curacao
1 pony French Vermouth
1 pony fresh cream

Beauty Spot

2/3 Dry Gin
1/3 Grenadine
1 white of egg

Ladies Delight

1/2 jigger Gin
1/2 jigger Orange Juice
1 dash Curacao
1 dash Lemon Juice
1/2 teaspoon sugar

Love

1 jigger Sloe Gin
1 white of egg
2 dashes Lemon Juice
2 dashes Raspberry Juice

Alexander's Sister

1 pony Dry Gin
1 pony Creme de Menthe
1 pony fresh cream

Jack Rose

2/3 Applejack
1/3 Grenadine Syrup
1 Lime (juice only)

Blue Devil

1/2 Dry Gin
1/4 Lemon or Lime Juice
1/4 Maraschino
2 dashes Creme de Yvette

POLLYANNA

3 SLICES ORANGE
3 SLICES PINEAPPLE
  (MUDDLE THESE THOROUGHLY)
1 JIGGER DRY GIN
1/2 JIGGER ITALIAN VERMOUTH
2 DASHES GRENADINE

CLOVER CLUB #1

1 JIGGER GIN
3 DASHES RASPBERRY SYRUP
1 WHITE OF EGG
1/2 TEASPOON SUGAR
1/2 LEMON (JUICE ONLY)
SHAKE WELL WITH ICE.

CLOVER CLUB #2

1 JIGGER GIN
1 DASH GRENADINE
1 WHITE OF EGG
1 LEMON (JUICE ONLY)

CLOVER LEAF

1 JIGGER DRY GIN
1 PONY ITALIAN VERMOUTH
1 WHITE OF EGG
1/2 LEMON (JUICE ONLY)
1 DASH GRENADINE
SERVE WITH A MINT LEAF.

WATERBURY

1 JIGGER BRANDY
1 WHITE OF EGG
1/2 LIME (JUICE ONLY)
1/2 TEASPOON POWDERED SUGAR
2 DASHES GRENADINE

COVINGTON

1/2 JIGGER BOURBON
1/2 JIGGER PORT WINE
1/4 LEMON (JUICE ONLY)
1/2 TEASPOON SUGAR
1 WHITE OF EGG
SERVE WITH SLICE OF PINEAPPLE

PINK LADY

1/3 GIN
1/3 LIME JUICE
1/3 APPLEJACK
2 DASHES GRENADINE

SNICKER

1 PONY DRY GIN
1/2 PONY FRENCH VERMOUTH
1 WHITE OF EGG
2 DASHES MARASCHINO
1 TEASPOON SYRUP
1 DASH ORANGE BITTERS

HERE'S TO A LONG LIFE AND A MERRY ONE,
  A QUICK DEATH AND A HAPPY ONE,
A GOOD GIRL AND A PRETTY ONE,
  A COLD BOTTLE AND ANOTHER ONE.
                    – CLOVER CLUB TOAST

"EPICUREAN" COCKTAILS

There are also scores of cocktails—some authorities on "mixology" question their right to that classification—of which the countless array of tempting cordials form the base.

These are especially attractive to the epicure because they afford him such an endless variety in delicacy of taste. And why shouldn't they? Just stop to think that Benedictine, perhaps the oldest and best known liqueur is said to be a distillation of the choicest Cognac and over eighty varieties of spices and herbs, flowers and roots. And Chartreuse, another of the famous cordials, is supposed to have almost as many ingredients.

Whether the fact that both of these liqueurs were originally made in monasteries has anything to do with their goodness is beside the point. (Benedictine was actually brought to perfection by Friar Benedict, the founder of the order that bears his name). That they are good is beyond dispute, and they—as well as the countless other cordials that vie with them in the tempting tastes of Curacao, Kummel, Creme de Cacao, Cointreau, etc.—lend popularity to many drinks.

Some of these—we cannot even pretend that we are scratching the surface—are in the following list:—

JUST Cocktails

Between the Sheets

1/3 Cointreau
1/3 Benedictine
1/3 Brandy

Stinger

1/2 White Creme de Menthe
1/2 Brandy

Queen Elizabeth

1/3 Benedictine
1/2 Lime (juice only)
2/3 French Vermouth

Bohemian Girl

1 Jigger Creme de Cacao
1 Jigger Brandy
1 White of Egg
1/2 Lime (juice only)

Dream

1/3 Curacao
2/3 Brandy
1 dash Absinthe

Snowball

1/3 Gin
1/6 Creme de Violette
1/6 White Creme de Menthe
1/6 Anisette
1/6 Fresh Cream

Prince George

1/3 Grand Marnier
2/3 Bacardi
1/2 Lime (juice only)
Twist of Lemon peel.

Kretchma

2/5 Vodka
2/5 Creme de Cacao
1/5 Lemon juice
1 dash Grenadine

White Lady

2/3 Cointreau
1/6 Creme de Menthe
1/6 Brandy

Xanthia

1/3 Cherry Brandy
1/3 Yellow Chartreuse
1/3 Gin

Maiden's Kiss

1/5 Creme de Roses
1/5 Curacao
1/5 Maraschino
1/5 Yellow Chartreuse
1/5 Benedictine

ANGEL'S KISS

1/4 CREME DE CACAO
1/4 BRANDY
1/4 CREME DE YVETTE
1/4 FRESH CREAM
POUR CAREFULLY, SO THAT
  INGREDIENTS DO NOT MIX,
  USING POUSSE CAFE GLASS.

YELLOW PARROT

1/3 BRANDY
1/3 YELLOW CHARTREUSE
1/3 ANISETTE

PING PONG

1/2 SLOE GIN
1/2 CREME DE YVETTE
1/4 LEMON (JUICE ONLY)
1 WHITE OF EGG

CHRYSANTHEMUM

1/2 BENEDICTINE
1/2 FRENCH VERMOUTH
3 DASHES ABSINTHE

SWISSESSE

1 JIGGER ABSINTHE
1/2 JIGGER ANISETTE
1 WHITE OF EGG

ST. PATRICK'S DAY

1/3 GREEN CREME DE MENTHE
1/3 GREEN CHARTREUSE
1/3 IRISH WHISKEY
1 DASH BITTERS
(ANY KIND EXCEPT ORANGE)

BENEDICTINE

1 PONY BENEDICTINE
1 PONY FRENCH VERMOUTH
1/2 PONY LIME JUICE

SWEET MARIE

1/5 BENEDICTINE
1/5 CURACAO
1/5 BRANDY
1/5 CHARTREUSE
1/5 FRESH CREAM

FORGET ME NOT

1/5 CHARTREUSE
1/5 MARASCHINO
1/5 BRANDY
1/5 CURACAO
1/5 FRESH CREAM

CONEY ISLE

1/4 CURACAO
1/4 CHARTREUSE
1/4 ABSINTHE
1/4 FRESH CREAM

ENCHANTED ISLAND

1 JIGGER BOURBON
1/2 JIGGER CREME DE CACAO
1 PONY FRESH CREAM
4 DASHES GRENADINE

TROPICAL

1/3 CREME DE CACAO
1/3 MARASCHINO
1/3 FRENCH VERMOUTH
1 DASH BITTERS

VIRGIN

1/3 FORBIDDEN FRUIT
1/3 WHITE CREME DE MENTHE
1/3 GIN
SHAKE WELL AND STRAIN.

CLOVEN HOOF

1/2 BRANDY
1/2 CREME DE MENTHE
1 DASH ABSINTHE

QUELLE VIE

1/3 KUMMEL
2/3 BRANDY

SIDE CAR

2/3 BRANDY
1/3 COINTREAU
1 DASH LIME JUICE

GYPSY

2/3 VODKA
1/3 BENEDICTINE
1 DASH BITTERS

DOLORES

1/3 CREME DE CACAO
1/3 CHERRY BRANDY
1/3 SPANISH BRANDY
1 WHITE OF EGG

WIDOW'S KISS

1/3 BENEDICTINE
1/3 PARFAIT D'AMOUR
1/3 YELLOW CHARTREUSE
1 WHITE OF EGG
   (FLOAT ON TOP)

MABEL BERRA

1/2 JIGGER SWEDISH PUNCH
1/2 JIGGER SLOE GIN
1/2 LIME (JUICE ONLY)

RUSSIAN

1/3 CREME DE CACAO
1/3 VODKA
1/3 DRY GIN

MERRY WIDOW

1/2 MARASCHINO
1/2 CHERRY BRANDY
STIR WELL WITH ICE AND
    SERVE WITH A CHERRY.

WIDOW'S DREAM

1 JIGGER BENEDICTINE
1 WHOLE EGG
SHAKE WELL, FLOAT ONE
    TABLESPOON CREAM ON
    TOP.

CASTLE DIP

1/2 WHITE CREME DE MENTHE
1/2 APPLE BRANDY
3 DASHES ABSINTHE

APPARENT

1 JIGGER CREME DE CACAO
1 JIGGER DRY GIN
1 DASH ABSINTHE

YELLOW DAISY

1 PONY GRAND MARNIER
1 PONY DRY GIN
1 PONY FRENCH VERMOUTH
1 DASH ANISETTE
SERVE WITH A CHERRY.

ROYAL SMILE

2 PONIES APPLE BRANDY
1 PONY DRY GIN
1/4 LEMON (JUICE ONLY)
2 DASHES GRENADINE

UNION JACK

1 PONY CREME DE YVETTE
2 PONIES DRY GIN
2 DASHES GRENADINE

JEWEL

1 PONY GREEN CHARTREUSE
1 PONY ITALIAN VERMOUTH
1 PONY DRY GIN
1 DASH ORANGE BITTERS

PANAMA

1 PONY CREME DE CACAO
1 PONY BRANDY
1 PONY FRESH CREAM

BLOCK & FALL

1/3 COINTREAU
1/6 ANISETTE
1/3 BRANDY
1/6 APPLEJACK

MORNING AFTER

2 JIGGERS ABSINTHE
1 TEASPOON ANISETTE SYRUP
1 WHITE OF EGG
1 DASH OF SODA (ON TOP)

DIANA

3/4 WHITE CREME DE MENTHE
1/4 COGNAC
FILL COCKTAIL GLASS WITH
    SHAVED ICE AND POUR THE
    ABOVE OVER IT.

PLUIE D'OR

1/3 VIELLE CURE
1/3 GIN
1/6 CURACAO
1/6 KUMMEL

GRENADINE

1/3 OXYGENE CUSENIER
1/3 WHITE CREME DE MENTHE
1/3 GIN
1 TEASPOON FRAMBOISE SYRUP
SHAKE WELL AND STRAIN.

NIGHT CAP

1/3 ANISETTE
1/3 CURACAO
1/3 BRANDY
1 YOLK OF EGG

AFTER SUPPER

1 PONY COGNAC
1 PONY CURACAO
4 DASHES LEMON JUICE

CANADIAN

1 JIGGER CURACAO
3 DASHES JAMAICA RUM
1/2 LEMON (JUICE ONLY)
1/4 TABLESPOON POWDERED SUGAR

BUTTON HOOK

1/4 WHITE CREME DE MENTHE
1/4 ABSINTHE
1/4 APRICOT BRANDY
1/4 COGNAC

CHOCOLATE

1/3 MARASCHINO
1/3 BLACKBERRY LIQUEUR
1/3 YELLOW CHARTREUSE
1 YOLK OF EGG

DIAMOND LIL

1/5 CURACAO
1/5 RUM
1/5 ABSINTHE
1/5 CREME DE YVETTE
1/5 GRENADINE

VOLSTEAD

1/3 Swedish Punch
1/3 Rye
1/6 Orange Juice
1/6 Raspberry Syrup
1 dash Anisette

VALENCIA

2/3 Apricot Brandy
1/3 Orange Juice
2 dashes Orange Bitters

ETHEL DUFFY

1 pony White Creme de Menthe
1 pony Brandy
1 pony White Curacao

SMILE

1 jigger Grenadine
1 jigger Gin
2 dashes Lemon Juice

ASTORIA QUEEN

1/4 Brandy
1/4 Curacao
1/4 Maraschino
1/4 Fresh Cream

AMER PICON

1 jigger Dry Gin
1 pony Amer Picon
3 dashes Grenadine

ULYSSES

1/3 Cherry Brandy
1/3 French Vermouth
1/3 Cognac
1 Orange peel, squeezed

LASKY

1 pony Swedish Punch
1 pony Grape Juice
1 pony Gin

Say, why did Time,
  His glass sublime,
    Fill up with sand unsightly,
When wine he knew,
  Runs brisker through,
    And sparkles far more brightly?
          — Moore

—THEN WE HAVE THE
"FAVORITE SONS"

Of course there are cocktails without end that were first mixed
by or named after some celebrity, usually a native of the city or
state where the drink had its birth. Often these do not have
enough appeal to the palate to earn for them more than a local
and sentimental popularity, but there are some exceptions to this
rule.

For instance, the Sazerac cocktail was born in New Orleans, and
christened after one of the daring blades of that historic city's
Creole days, but it has come to be fairly popular from coast to
coast. It has surely earned the right to head a group of cocktails
that might be aptly designated the "favorite son" class, for they
usually get the votes of only their home town constituency.

A call for one of these will almost invariably bring a blank stare
to the face of your friend the bartender, but they are good and
certainly deserving of more renown.

> If you don't find your especial pet in this group, turn
> to the back of the book and write it down on the
> blank page provided for just that purpose.

JUST
Cocktails

SAZERAC

1 JIGGER BOURBON OR SCOTCH
1 DASH ABSINTHE
1 DASH ITALIAN VERMOUTH
ADD A FEW DASHES OF
  PEYCHAND BITTERS.

CUBAN

2/3 BRANDY
1/3 APRICOT BRANDY
1/2 LIME (JUICE ONLY)

PALM BEACH

1/3 BACARDI RUM
1/3 GORDON WATER
1/3 PINEAPPLE JUICE

EVE'S APPLE

1/3 APPLEJACK
1/3 GRAPEFRUIT JUICE
1/3 GALDRIC PUNCH

MOUNTAIN

1 JIGGER BOURBON WHISKEY
1 DASH LEMON JUICE
1 DASH ITALIAN VERMOUTH
1 DASH FRENCH VERMOUTH
1 WHITE OF EGG

YELLOW RATTLER

1/4 DRY GIN
1/4 ITALIAN VERMOUTH
1/4 FRENCH VERMOUTH
1/4 ORANGE JUICE

DEAUVILLE

1/4 FINE COGNAC
1/4 APPLE BRANDY
1/4 COINTREAU
1/4 LEMON JUICE

ENGLISH ROSE

1/2 DRY GIN
1/4 COGNAC
1/4 FRENCH VERMOUTH
4 DASHES GRENADINE
1 DASH LEMON JUICE
RUB THE RIM OF GLASS WITH
  LEMON AND DIP IN POWDERED
  SUGAR.

BENNETT

1 WINEGLASS DRY GIN
1/2 LIME (JUICE ONLY)
1/2 TEASPOON POWDERED SUGAR
2 DASHES BITTERS

SEPTEMBER MORN

1 JIGGER RUM
1/2 LIME (JUICE ONLY)
3 DASHES GRENADINE
1 WHITE OF EGG

CATASTROPHE

1 JIGGER COGNAC
1/2 JIGGER APPLEJACK
1/2 JIGGER BENEDICTINE
2 DASHES ABSINTHE

RACQUET CLUB

1 WINEGLASS DRY GIN
1 PONY FRENCH VERMOUTH
1 DASH ORANGE BITTERS

OPERA

2 PONIES DRY GIN
1/2 PONY DUBONNET
1/2 PONY MARASCHINO

LADIES'

1 JIGGER BOURBON
2 DASHES ABSINTHE
3 DASHES ANISETTE
2 DASHES BITTERS
SERVE WITH A SLICE
   OF PINEAPPLE.

HOLLAND HOUSE

1 JIGGER DRY GIN
1/2 JIGGER FRENCH VERMOUTH
1/4 LEMON (JUICE ONLY)
4 DASHES MARASCHINO
1 SLICE PINEAPPLE

KNOCK-OUT

1 PONY ABSINTHE
1 PONY FRENCH VERMOUTH
1 PONY DRY GIN
1 TEASPOON WHITE CREME DE MENTHE
SERVE WITH A CHERRY

BOOSTER

1 JIGGER BRANDY
1 WHITE OF EGG
4 DASHES CURACAO
SERVE WITH GRATED NUTMEG
   ON TOP.

VANDERBILT HOTEL

1 JIGGER COGNAC
1/2 PONY CHERRY BRANDY
3 DASHES SYRUP
2 DASHES BITTERS

SAVOY TANGO

1 JIGGER SLOE GIN
1 JIGGER APPLEJACK

TWIN SIX

1 JIGGER DRY GIN
1/2 JIGGER ITALIAN VERMOUTH
1/4 ORANGE (JUICE ONLY)
1 WHITE OF EGG
1 DASH GRENADINE

WHIP

1 PONY BRANDY
1/2 PONY FRENCH VERMOUTH
1/2 PONY ITALIAN VERMOUTH
1 DASH ABSINTHE
3 DASHES CURACAO

BELMONT

2 PONIES DRY GIN
1 PONY RASPBERRY SYRUP
1 PONY FRESH CREAM

ALLIES

1 JIGGER DRY GIN
1 JIGGER FRENCH VERMOUTH
2 DASHES RUSSIAN KUMMEL

WHISKEY APPETIZER

1 JIGGER BOURBON
2 DASHES BITTERS
3 DASHES CURACAO

ZAZA

1 JIGGER DRY GIN
1/2 JIGGER DUBONNET
1 PIECE ORANGE PEEL

MINNEHAHA

1 JIGGER DRY GIN
1/2 JIGGER ITALIAN VERMOUTH
1/2 JIGGER FRENCH VERMOUTH
1/4 ORANGE (JUICE ONLY)

LEAVE IT TO ME

1 1/2 JIGGERS GIN
1 TEASPOON RASPBERRY SYRUP
1 TEASPOON LEMON JUICE
1 DASH MARASCHINO

POLO

2/3 DRY GIN
1/6 ORANGE JUICE
1/6 GRAPEFRUIT JUICE

PLANTER'S

1/2 JAMAICA RUM
1/4 LEMON JUICE
1/4 SYRUP

WASHINGTON'S STIRRUP CUP

1 JIGGER BRANDY
1 JIGGER CHERRY BRANDY
1/2 LEMON (JUICE ONLY)

HAVE A HEART

1 JIGGER DRY GIN
1/2 JIGGER SWEDISH PUNCH
1/2 LIME (JUICE ONLY)
2 DASHES GRENADINE
SERVE WITH PINEAPPLE
    AND CHERRY.

Depth Bomb

1/2 Cognac
1/2 Apple Brandy
1 dash Lemon Juice
4 dashes Grenadine

Knickerbocker

2/3 Dry Gin
1/3 French Vermouth
1 dash Italian Vermouth
1 twist Lemon Peel

South Side

1 jigger Dry Gin
1/2 Lemon (juice only)
1 teaspoon Sugar
3 Mint Leaves

South Side (Irvin Cobb's)

1 jigger Dry Gin
1 dash Curacao
1 Lime (juice only)
2 Mint Leaves
("On a warm day this
South Side is as re-
freshing as the north
side of a shade tree"
   -Cobb)

Saratoga

1 jigger Brandy
2 dashes Maraschino
2 dashes Pineapple Juice
1 dash Orange Bitters

Moulin Rouge

1/3 Italian Vermouth
2/3 Sloe Gin
1 dash Pernod

Flamingo

1 jigger Dry Gin
1/2 pony Brandy
1/2 Lime (juice only)
3 dashes Grenadine

Harry Lauder

1/2 Scotch Whiskey
1/2 Italian Vermouth
2 dashes Gum Syrup

Number One

1 jigger Old Tom Gin
1 pony Italian Vermouth
1 twist Lemon Peel

Smiler

1 jigger Dry Gin
1/2 jigger French Vermouth
1/2 jigger Italian Vermouth
1 dash Bitters
1 dash Orange Juice

FINE AND DANDY

1/2 DRY GIN
1/4 COINTREAU
1/4 LEMON JUICE
1 DASH BITTERS
SERVE WITH A CHERRY.

BILTMORE

1 PIECE FRESH PINEAPPLE
  (MUDDLED)
1 JIGGER DRY GIN
1/2 PONY ITALIAN VERMOUTH
1 DASH MARASCHINO
SERVE WITH A HAZEL NUT,
  PRESERVED IN MARASCHINO.

MALLORY

1/2 PONY COGNAC
1/2 PONY CREME DE MENTHE
1/2 PONY APRICOT BRANDY
2 DASHES ABSINTHE

OLD PAL

1/3 WHISKEY
1/3 CREME DE MENTHE
1/3 FRENCH VERMOUTH

NEVADA

1 JIGGER RUM
1/2 GRAPEFRUIT (JUICE ONLY)
1 LIME (JUICE ONLY)
1 DASH BITTERS
1 TEASPOON POWDERED SUGAR

DELMONICA SPECIAL

1 PONY GIN
1/2 PONY FRENCH VERMOUTH
1/2 PONY ITALIAN VERMOUTH
1 PONY BRANDY
3 DASHES ANGOSTURA BITTERS
1 TWIST LEMON PEEL

POPPY

2/3 DRY GIN
1/3 CREME DE CACAO

APPLE PIE

1/2 RUM
1/2 ITALIAN VERMOUTH
4 DASHES BRANDY
2 DASHES GRENADINE
4 DASHES LEMON JUICE

AFTER DINNER

1 JIGGER COGNAC
1 JIGGER CURACAO

SOUL KISS

1/3 WHISKEY
1/3 FRENCH VERMOUTH
1/6 ORANGE JUICE
1/6 DUBONNET

Shamrock

1/2 Irish Whiskey
1/2 French Vermouth
3 dashes Chartreuse (green)
3 dashes Creme de Menthe
Serve with an olive

Creole Lady

1 jigger Whiskey
1 jigger Madeira Wine
3 dashes Grenadine
Serve with two cherries

Jockey Club

1 jigger Dry Gin
4 dashes Lemon Juice
2 dashes Creme de Cacao
1 dash Bitters

Golden Slipper

1 jigger Cognac
1 dash Yellow Chartreuse
1 yolk of egg
Float egg yolk. Do not
    shake.

Little Devil

1/6 Lemon Juice
1/6 Cointreau
1/3 Rum
1/3 Dry Gin

Chelsea Side Car

1 pony Cointreau
1 pony Dry Gin
1 pony Lemon Juice

Hawaiian

2 ponies Dry Gin
1 pony Pineapple Juice
1 pony Curacao

Morning

1 pony Brandy
1 pony French Vermouth
2 dashes Curacao
2 dashes Absinthe
2 dashes Orange Bitters
2 dashes Maraschino

Rolls Royce

1/4 French Vermouth
1/4 Italian Vermouth
1/2 Dry Gin
1 dash Benedictine

Income Tax

1/2 Dry Gin
1/4 French Vermouth
1/4 Italian Vermouth
1 dash Bitters
1/4 Orange (Juice only)

GOLDEN DAWN

1/4 APPLEJACK
1/4 APRICOT BRANDY
1/4 DRY GIN
1/4 ORANGE JUICE

GRAPEFRUIT

1 JIGGER DRY GIN
1 JIGGER GRAPEFRUIT JUICE
2 DASHES SYRUP

CLUB

1 JIGGER DRY GIN
3 DASHES RUM
3 DASHES ORANGE BITTERS
1 DASH GREEN CHARTREUSE

CLUB (NEW ENG-
LAND STYLE

2/3 DRY GIN
1/3 ITALIAN VERMOUTH
SERVE WITH AN OLIVE.

CHAMPAGNE (AS
SERVED AT THE COP-
LEY PLAZA IN BOS-
TON)

1 LUMP SUGAR
2 DASHES ANGOSTURA BITTERS
  (SATURATE THE SUGAR WITH
  THIS)
1 PIECE LEMON PEEL
USE FIVE OUNCE STEM GLASS
  AND FILL WITH CHAMPAGNE.

CORNELL

1 JIGGER DRY GIN
1 WHITE OF EGG
3 DASHES MARASCHINO
2 DASHES LEMON JUICE

YALE

1 JIGGER DRY GIN
1/2 JIGGER FRENCH VERMOUTH
3 DASHES CREME DE YVETTE
1 DASH BITTERS

PRINCETON

1 JIGGER DRY GIN
1 JIGGER FRENCH VERMOUTH
2 DASHES LIME JUICE
SERVE WITH AN OLIVE.

HARVARD

1 JIGGER BRANDY
1 JIGGER ITALIAN VERMOUTH
1 DASH BITTERS
3 DASHES GRENADINE

PETER PAN

1/4 BITTERS
1/4 ORANGE JUICE
1/4 FRENCH VERMOUTH
1/4 DRY GIN

JACK RABBIT

1/3 Dry Gin
1/3 French Vermouth
1/6 Brandy
1/6 Cointreau

Abbey

1 jigger Dry Gin
1/2 jigger Orange Juice
1 dash Bitters
Serve with a cherry.

Zazarac

1 jigger Bourbon
1 dash Rum
1 dash Anisette
1 dash Gum Syrup
1 dash Bitters
3 dashes Absinthe

Sir Walter (Swalter

1 pony Brandy
1 pony Rum
1 teaspoon Grenadine
1 teaspoon Lemon Juice
1 teaspoon Curacao

Harlem

2/3 Dry Gin
1/3 Pineapple Juice
3 dashes Maraschino
Serve with Pineapple cubes

Pall Mall

1/3 Italian Vermouth
1/3 French Vermouth
1/3 Dry Gin
1 dash Orange Bitters
1 teaspoon White Creme de Menthe

Blue Train

1 jigger Cognac
1 pony Pineapple Juice
Shake with cracked ice and
   pour into Champagne glass.
   Fill with Champagne, stir
   gently, and serve at once.

White Way

1 wineglass Dry Gin
1 pony White Creme de Menthe

Poker

1 jigger Rum
1 jigger Italian Vermouth

Everybody's Irish

1 jigger Irish Whiskey
6 dashes Green Chartreuse
3 dashes Green Creme de Menthe
1 green Olive

DEMPSEY

1/2 DRY GIN
1/2 APPLE BRANDY
2 DASHES ABSINTHE
2 DASHES GRENADINE

COLD DECK

1/2 BRANDY
1/4 WHITE CREME DE MENTHE
1/4 ITALIAN VERMOUTH

WESTERN ROSE

1 JIGGER DRY GIN
1/2 JIGGER BRANDY
1/2 JIGGER FRENCH VERMOUTH
1 DASH LEMON JUICE

LA REGENCE

1/4 GIN
1/4 BRANDY
1/4 COINTREAU
1/4 ITALIAN VERMOUTH

WASHINGTON

1 PONY FRENCH VERMOUTH
1/2 PONY BRANDY
3 DASHES ANGOSTURA BITTERS
3 DASHES GUM SYRUP

KENTUCKY RIVER

3/4 BOURBON WHISKEY
1/4 CREME DE CACAO
4 DASHES PEACH BITTERS
1 TWIST LEMON PEEL

CASINO

1 1/2 JIGGERS DRY GIN
2 DASHES MARASCHINO
2 DASHES ORANGE BITTERS
2 DASHES LEMON JUICE
SERVE WITH A CHERRY.

APPLEJACK #1

1 JIGGER APPLEJACK
3 DASHES RASPBERRY SYRUP
3 DASHES GUM SYRUP

APPLEJACK #2

1 PONY APPLEJACK
1 PONY ITALIAN VERMOUTH
1 DASH ANGOSTURA BITTERS

BAMBOO

1/2 DRY SHERRY
1/2 ITALIAN VERMOUTH

QUAKER

1 PONY BRANDY
1 PONY RUM
1/2 PONY LEMON JUICE
1/2 PONY RASPBERRY SYRUP

The Cowboy

2/3 Scotch
1/3 Fresh Cream
Add cracked ice and
    shake well.

Gray Dawn

1 Jigger Gin
1 White of Egg
1 Spoonful Worcestershire

Black Eye

1/2 Scotch
1/2 Fresh Cream
3 Dashes Creme de Cacao

Rob Roy

2/3 Scotch
1/3 Italian Vermouth
1 Dash Bitters

Cherry Blossom

1 Pony Cognac
1 Pony Cherry Brandy
1 Dash Curacao
1 Dash Lemon Juice
1 Dash Grenadine

Appetizer

1 Pony Dry Gin
1 Pony Dubonnet
1/2 Orange (Juice Only)

Alfonso

1 Pony Creme de Cacao
2 Dashes Bitters
1 Lump Sugar
1 Piece Ice
Stir gently, pour into
    Champagne glass, fill
    with Champagne.

Elk's Own

1 Jigger Whiskey
1/2 Jigger Port Wine
1 White of Egg
1/2 Lemon (Juice Only)
1 Teaspoon Sugar
Serve with a slice
    of Pineapple

Lone Tree

1/2 Tom Gin
1/4 Italian Vermouth
1/4 French Vermouth

Honeymoon

1 Pony Benedictine
1 Pony Apple Brandy
1/2 Lemon (Juice Only)
3 Dashes Curacao

SKYROCKET

1 PONY WHISKEY
1 PONY SWEDISH PUNCH
1 PONY FRENCH VERMOUTH
1 DASH LEMON JUICE
1 DASH BITTERS

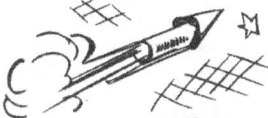

PARISIAN BLONDE

1 PONY JAMAICA RUM
1 PONY CURACAO
1 PONY FRESH CREAM

MAIDEN'S BLUSH

1 JIGGER DRY GIN
1 DASH LEMON JUICE
4 DASHES ORANGE CURACAO
4 DASHES GRENADINE

LIBERTY

1 JIGGER APPLEJACK
1/2 JIGGER JAMAICA RUM
1 DASH SYRUP

THIRD RAIL

1 PONY APPLEJACK
1 PONY RUM
1 PONY COGNAC
1 DASH ABSINTHE

SHRINER

1 PONY BRANDY
1 PONY SLOE GIN
2 DASHES BITTERS
2 DASHES GUM SYRUP
1 TWIST LEMON PEEL

SEVILLA

1 PONY PORT WINE
1 PONY JAMAICA RUM
1 WHOLE EGG
1/2 TEASPOON POWDERED SUGAR

LONDON

1 WINEGLASS DRY GIN
2 DASHES ORANGE BITTERS
2 DASHES SYRUP
2 DASHES MARASCHINO
1 TWIST LEMON PEEL

IMPERIAL

1 JIGGER FRENCH VERMOUTH
1 JIGGER DRY GIN
1 DASH MARASCHINO
1 DASH BITTERS

EYE OPENER

1 JIGGER RUM
1 YOLK OF EGG
1 TEASPOON POWDERED SUGAR
2 DASHES ABSINTHE
2 DASHES CURACAO
2 DASHES CREME DE CACAO

WEDDING BELLE

1 PONY DRY GIN
1 PONY DUBONNET
1/2 PONY CHERRY BRANDY
1/4 ORANGE (JUICE ONLY)

DU BARRY

2/3 DRY GIN
1/3 FRENCH VERMOUTH
1 DASH BITTERS
2 DASHES ABSINTHE
SERVE WITH SLICE OF ORANGE

FRANKENJACK

1 PONY DRY GIN
1 PONY FRENCH VERMOUTH
1/2 PONY COINTREAU
1/2 PONY BRANDY
SERVE WITH A CHERRY

BOSTON

1/4 DRY GIN
1/4 BRANDY
1/4 LEMON JUICE
1/4 GRENADINE

BLOODHOUND

1/2 DRY GIN
1/4 FRENCH VERMOUTH
1/4 ITALIAN VERMOUTH
2 OR 3 CRUSHED STRAWBERRIES

BOLERO

2/3 JAMAICA RUM
1/3 APPLEJACK
2 DASHES ITALIAN VERMOUTH

FLYING SCOTCHMAN

1/2 JIGGER SCOTCH WHISKEY
1/2 JIGGER ITALIAN VERMOUTH
1 DASH BITTERS
1 DASH SYRUP

SWISS FAMILY

2/3 BOURBON WHISKEY
1/3 FRENCH VERMOUTH
2 DASHES PERNOD
2 DASHES ANGOSTURA BITTERS

LOS ANGELES

1 JIGGER WHISKEY
1 LEMON (JUICE ONLY)
1 TEASPOON SUGAR
1 WHOLE EGG
1 DASH ITALIAN VERMOUTH

POLAR

1 PONY DRY GIN
1 PONY MARASCHINO
1/2 LEMON (JUICE ONLY)
1 WHITE OF EGG

BROKEN SPUR

2/3 PORT WINE
1/6 DRY GIN
1/6 ITALIAN VERMOUTH
1 YOLK OF EGG
1 TEASPOON ANISETTE

BRONX GOLDEN

1/2 DRY GIN
1/4 FRENCH VERMOUTH
1/4 ITALIAN VERMOUTH
1 TEASPOON ORANGE JUICE
1 YOLK OF EGG

BRONX SILVER

1 JIGGER DRY GIN
1/2 JIGGER FRENCH VERMOUTH
1 TEASPOON ORANGE JUICE
1 WHITE OF EGG

BULL DOG

1 JIGGER CHERRY BRANDY
1/2 JIGGER DRY GIN
1/2 LIME (JUICE ONLY)

ZULU

1/2 JIGGER DRY GIN
1/2 JIGGER CHERRY BRANDY
2 DASHES ANGOSTURA BITTERS

KENTUCKY COLONEL

1 JIGGER BOURBON WHISKEY
1/2 PONY BENEDICTINE
SERVE WITH A TWIST OF LEMON
   PEEL IN AN OLD FASHIONED
   GLASS.

NEW YORK

1 JIGGER WHISKEY
1 LIME (JUICE ONLY)
1/2 TEASPOON POWDERED SUGAR
2 DASHES GRENADINE
1 SLICE ORANGE PEEL

ADONIS

2/3 DRY SHERRY
1/3 ITALIAN VERMOUTH
1 DASH ORANGE BITTERS

SUNSHINE

1 PONY PINEAPPLE JUICE
1 PONY BACARDI RUM
1 PONY FRENCH VERMOUTH
1 DASH GRENADINE

TEMPTATION

1 JIGGER BOURBON
2 DASHES CURACAO
2 DASHES ABSINTHE
2 DASHES DUBONNET
1 PIECE ORANGE PEEL
1 PIECE LEMON PEEL

Corpse Reviver

1 jigger Cognac
1/2 jigger Apple Brandy
1/2 jigger Italian Vermouth

Hop Toad

1 1/2 jiggers Brandy
1/2 jigger Lemon juice

B.V.D.

1 pony Jamaica Rum
1 pony Dry Gin
1 pony French Vermouth

Flag

1/2 jigger Brandy
4 dashes Orange Curacao
Pour one tablespoon Creme de
   Yvette into 4 oz. cocktail
   glass, add the above after
   shaking, top with Claret.

Gilroy

1 pony Brandy
1 pony Dry Gin
1/2 pony French Vermouth
1/2 pony Lemon juice
1 dash Orange Bitters

Damn-the-Weather

1 jigger Dry Gin
1/2 jigger Italian Vermouth
1/2 jigger Orange juice
3 dashes Curacao

Devil's

1 jigger Port Wine
1 jigger French Vermouth
2 dashes Lemon juice

T.N.T.

1 jigger Whiskey
1 jigger Absinthe

Up to Date

1 jigger Sherry Wine
1 jigger Whiskey
2 dashes Grand Marnier
2 dashes Bitters

Dixie

1 pony Dry Gin
1/2 pony Absinthe
1/2 pony French Vermouth
1/2 Orange (juice only)

Seventh Heaven

1 wineglass Dry Gin
1/2 pony Maraschino
1/2 pony Grapefruit juice
Serve with a sprig of fresh
   mint.

ECLIPSE

1/3 DRY GIN
2/3 SLOE GIN
2 DASHES LEMON JUICE
PUT ENOUGH GRENADINE IN
  GLASS TO COVER A RIPE
  OLIVE. SHAKE THE GIN,
  LEMON JUICE AND ICE
  WELL, THEN STRAIN IT
  GENTLY OVER THE GREN-
  ADINE SO THAT IT DOES
  NOT MIX.

GOOD TIMES

2/3 TOM GIN
1/3 FRENCH VERMOUTH
1 TWIST OF LEMON PEEL

AVIATION

1 JIGGER APPLEJACK
1/2 LIME (JUICE ONLY)
1 DASH ABSINTHE
1 BARSPOON GRENADINE

PICK-ME-UP

1 JIGGER COGNAC
1/2 LEMON (JUICE ONLY)
1 TEASPOON GRENADINE
STRAIN INTO CHAMPAGNE GLASS
  AND FILL BALANCE WITH
  CHAMPAGNE.

MAYFAIR

1/2 DRY GIN
1/4 BRANDY
1/4 ORANGE JUICE
1 DASH CLOVE SYRUP

ORIENTAL

1/2 JIGGER WHISKEY
1/4 JIGGER WHITE CURACAO
1/4 JIGGER ITALIAN VERMOUTH
1/2 LIME (JUICE ONLY)

RUM MANHATTAN

1 JIGGER RUM
1/2 JIGGER ITALIAN VERMOUTH
1 DASH BITTERS

CHINESE

2/3 JAMAICA RUM
1/3 GRENADINE
1 DASH BITTERS
3 DASHES MARASCHINO
3 DASHES CURACAO

BRANDY BLAZER

2 JIGGERS BRANDY
1 LUMP SUGAR
1 PIECE ORANGE PEEL
1 PIECE LEMON PEEL
USE HOT WHISKEY GLASS,
  STIR, AND LIGHT WITH
  A MATCH.

SHANGHAI

1 JIGGER JAMAICA RUM
1 PONY LEMON JUICE
4 DASHES ANISETTE
2 DASHES GRENADINE

TIPPERARY

1 PONY IRISH WHISKEY
1 PONY GREEN CHARTREUSE
1 PONY ITALIAN VERMOUTH

THUNDER CLAP

1 PONY BRANDY
1 PONY DRY GIN
1 PONY BOURBON

PLAZA

1/3 DRY GIN
1/3 FRENCH VERMOUTH
1/3 ITALIAN VERMOUTH
1 SLICE PINEAPPLE

FAIR & WARMER

2 PONIES JAMAICA RUM
1 PONY ITALIAN VERMOUTH
2 DASHES CURACAO

FALLEN ANGEL

1 JIGGER DRY GIN
1/2 LIME (JUICE ONLY)
2 DASHES CREME DE MENTHE
1 DASH BITTERS
SERVE WITH A CHERRY.

SAUCY SUE

1 WINEGLASS APPLEJACK
2 DASHES BRANDY
1 DASH ABSINTHE

HOFFMAN HOUSE

2 PONIES DRY GIN
1 PONY FRENCH VERMOUTH
2 DASHES ORANGE BITTERS
SERVE WITH OLIVE

KISS IN THE DARK

1 PONY CHERRY LIQUEUR
1 PONY GIN
1 PONY FRENCH VERMOUTH

BRANDY GUMP

1 JIGGER BRANDY
1 LEMON (JUICE ONLY)
2 DASHES GRENADINE

COMMODORE

1/3 BOURBON
1/3 CREME DE CACAO
1/3 LEMON JUICE
1 DASH GRENADINE
SERVE IN CHAMPAGNE GLASS

PINK ELEPHANT

2/3 DRY GIN
1/3 ITALIAN VERMOUTH
1 WHITE OF EGG
SHAKE WELL.

ASTORIA

2/3 SLOE GIN
1/3 FRENCH VERMOUTH
1 DASH ORANGE BITTERS

SLOEBERRY

1 JIGGER SLOE GIN
1 DASH ORANGE BITTERS

SHERRY

1 1/2 JIGGERS SHERRY
1 DASH ORANGE BITTERS
1 DASH ANGOSTURA BITTERS

MODERN #1

1 JIGGER SCOTCH WHISKEY
2 DASHES LEMON JUICE
1 DASH ABSINTHE
2 DASHES JAMAICA RUM
1 DASH ORANGE BITTERS

MODERN #2

2/3 SLOE GIN
1/3 SCOTCH WHISKEY
1 DASH PERNOD
1 DASH GRENADINE
1 DASH ORANGE BITTERS

FUTURITY

1/2 ITALIAN VERMOUTH
1/2 SLOE GIN
1 DASH ANGOSTURA BITTERS
2 DASHES GRENADINE

GOOD FELLOW

1/2 BOURBON WHISKEY
1/2 ITALIAN VERMOUTH
1 DASH ANGOSTURA BITTERS

MARCONI

2/3 APPLE BRANDY
1/3 ITALIAN VERMOUTH

BRIDAL

2/3 DRY GIN
1/3 ITALIAN VERMOUTH
1 DASH ORANGE BITTERS
1 DASH MARASCHINO
   ORANGE PEEL ON TOP.

FARMER'S

1/2 DRY GIN
1/4 ITALIAN VERMOUTH
1/4 FRENCH VERMOUTH
3 DASHES ANGOSTURA BITTERS

WARD EIGHT

1/2 Bourbon Whiskey
1/4 Lemon Juice
1/4 Orange Juice
1 dash Grenadine

MIAMI

1 pony Rum
1 pony Cointreau
3 dashes Lemon Juice

ROCK & RYE

1 Jigger Rock and Rye
1 pony Port Wine
1 dash Angostura Bitters
1 dash Lime Juice

BOBBY BURNS

3/4 Scotch Whiskey
1/4 Italian Vermouth
2 dashes Benedictine

WALDORF

1/3 Jigger Rye
1/3 Jigger Absinthe
1/3 Jigger Italian Vermouth
1 dash Bitters

BOMBAY

1 Jigger Brandy
1/2 Jigger French Vermouth
1/2 Jigger Italian Vermouth
1 dash Absinthe
2 dashes Curacao

WEEP NO MORE

1 Jigger Cognac
1 Jigger Dubonnet
1/2 Lime (Juice only)
1 dash Maraschino

LEAP YEAR

1 Wineglass Dry Gin
1/2 pony Grand Marnier
1/2 pony Italian Vermouth
1 dash Lemon Juice

CHAUNCEY

1/4 Rye
1/4 Gin
1/4 Brandy
1/4 Italian Vermouth
1 dash Orange Bitters

MAIDEN'S PRAYER

1 Jigger Dry Gin
1 dash Cointreau
1 dash Lemon Juice
1 dash Orange Juice

CORONATION

1/3 Italian Vermouth
1/3 French Vermouth
1/3 Applejack
1 dash Apricot Brandy

EARTHQUAKE

1/3 Gin
1/3 Absinthe
1/3 Scotch

BLUE MOON

2/3 Gin
1/3 French Vermouth
1 dash Orange Bitters
1 dash Creme Yvette

MONTE CRISTO

2/3 Cognac
1/3 Italian Vermouth

GOLDEN GATE

1/4 Gin
3/4 Orange Ice
Shake until melted

WEDDING BELLS

1/6 Cherry Brandy
1/6 Orange juice
1/3 Gin
1/3 Dubonnet

WARDAY'S

1 teaspoon Yellow Chartreuse
1/3 Applejack
1/3 Italian Vermouth
1/3 Gin

JAPALAC

1 jigger Rye
1 jigger French Vermouth
1/4 Orange (juice only)
1 dash Raspberry Syrup

LIBERAL

1/2 Rye
1/2 Italian Vermouth
3 dashes Amer Picon
1 dash Orange Bitters

BLACK HAWK

1/2 Rye
1/2 Sloe Gin

TANGO

1/2 Applejack
1/2 Sloe Gin

OASIS

2 ponies Sloe Gin
1 pony Grapefruit juice
   (unsweetened)

Journalist

1 wineglass Dry Gin
1/2 pony French Vermouth
1/2 pony Italian Vermouth
2 dashes Lemon Juice
2 dashes Curacao
1 dash Bitters

Blood and Sand

1 pony Scotch Whiskey
1 pony Cherry Brandy
1 pony Italian Vermouth
1/4 Orange (juice only)

Guard's

2 ponies Dry Gin
1 pony Italian Vermouth
2 dashes Curacao
Serve with a cherry

Saxon

1 jigger Jamaica Rum
1/2 Lime (juice only)
1 piece Orange peel
2 dashes Grenadine

French Rose

1 jigger Gin
1/2 jigger French Vermouth
1/2 jigger Cherry Liqueur

Sloppy Joe's

1 jigger Pineapple Juice
1/2 jigger Cognac
1/2 jigger Port Wine
1 dash Curacao
1 dash Grenadine

Classic

1 jigger Brandy
1/2 pony Curacao
1/2 pony Maraschino
1/2 pony Lemon Juice
Frost rim of glass with sugar

Fox River

1 jigger Bourbon
1/2 pony Creme de Cacao
4 dashes Bitters
Add piece of ice, stir well.

Green Room

1 jigger French Vermouth
1/2 jigger Brandy
2 dashes Curacao

Big Bad Wolf

2/3 Brandy
1/3 Curacao
1 yolk of egg
1 spoonful Grenadine

PREAKNESS

1/3 Italian Vermouth
2/3 Rye Whiskey
1 dash Angostura Bitters
2 dashes Benedictine
1 twist Lemon peel

EMERALD ISLE

1 jigger Dry Gin
1 teaspoon Creme de Menthe
3 dashes Bitters

X.Y.Z.

1/2 Jamaica Rum
1/4 Cointreau
1/4 Lemon juice

BALTIMORE BRACER

1/2 Anisette
1/2 Cognac
1 white of egg

ZANZIBAR

1/3 Dry Gin
1/3 French Vermouth
1/3 Lemon juice
1 dash Gum Syrup
1 dash Orange Bitters

COLONIAL

2/3 Dry Gin
1/3 Grapefruit juice
3 dashes Maraschino

SANTIAGO

2 dashes Grenadine
2 dashes Lemon juice
1 jigger Rum

AFFINITY

1/3 Scotch Whiskey
1/3 French Vermouth
1/3 Italian Vermouth

WALLICK

1 jigger Gin
1 jigger French Vermouth
3 dashes Curacao

TAILSPIN

1 pony Green Chartreuse
1 pony Italian Vermouth
1 pony Gin
1 dash Orange Bitters
1 twist Lemon peel
Serve with a cherry
    or olive.

FROTH BLOWER

1 jigger Gin
1 white of egg
1 teaspoon Grenadine

CAMERON'S KICK

1/3 SCOTCH WHISKEY
1/3 IRISH WHISKEY
1/6 LEMON JUICE
1/6 ORANGE BITTERS

CABARET

1 JIGGER DRY GIN
2 DASHES BITTERS
2 DASHES FRENCH VERMOUTH
2 DASHES BENEDICTINE
SERVE WITH A CHERRY

CARUSO

1/3 DRY GIN
1/3 FRENCH VERMOUTH
1/3 GREEN CREME DE MENTHE

BRAZIL

1/2 FRENCH VERMOUTH
1/2 SHERRY
1 DASH BITTERS
1 DASH ABSINTHE

BRAINSTORM

1 JIGGER IRISH WHISKEY
1 CUBE OF ICE
2 DASHES FRENCH VERMOUTH
2 DASHES BENEDICTINE
1 PIECE ORANGE PEEL
SERVE WITH BARSPOON IN OLD
FASHIONED GLASS.

ALASKA

3/4 DRY GIN
1/4 YELLOW CHARTREUSE
2 DASHES ORANGE BITTERS

BURMUDA ROSE

1/2 DRY GIN
1/4 BRANDY
1/4 GRENADINE

BARBARY COAST

1/4 DRY GIN
1/4 SCOTCH WHISKEY
1/4 CREME DE CACAO
1/4 FRESH CREAM

BOX CAR

1/2 JIGGER GIN
1/2 JIGGER COINTREAU
1/2 LIME (JUICE ONLY)
1 WHITE OF EGG
1 DASH GRENADINE
SERVE IN GLASS WITH
FROSTED RIM.

TURF

1/2 GIN
1/2 FRENCH VERMOUTH
2 DASHES ORANGE BITTERS
2 DASHES ABSINTHE
2 DASHES MARASCHINO
SERVE WITH AN OLIVE

BROWN UNIVERSITY

1/2 BOURBON WHISKEY
1/2 FRENCH VERMOUTH
2 DASHES ORANGE BITTERS

PAN AMERICAN

1 JIGGER RYE
1/2 LEMON (JUICE ONLY)
3 DASHES SYRUP

HONOLULU

1/3 BOURBON
1/3 FRENCH VERMOUTH
1/3 ITALIAN VERMOUTH

GREEN DRAGON

1/2 DRY GIN
1/4 CREME DE MENTHE
1/8 KUMMEL
1/8 LEMON JUICE
4 DASHES ORANGE BITTERS

SALOME

1/3 FRENCH VERMOUTH
1/3 DRY GIN
1/3 DUBONNET

HAVANA

2/3 PINEAPPLE JUICE
1/3 RUM
2 DASHES LEMON JUICE

THUNDER & LIGHTNING

1 JIGGER COGNAC
1 YOLK OF EGG
1 TEASPOON POWDERED SUGAR

CUPID

1 JIGGER SHERRY
1 FRESH EGG
1 TEASPOON SUGAR
ADD NUTMEG IN SERVING

CRYSTAL SLIPPER

3/4 DRY GIN
1/4 CREME DE YVETTE
2 DASHES ORANGE BITTERS

HURRICANE

1/3 WHISKEY
1/3 DRY GIN
1/3 CREME DE MENTHE
1/2 ORANGE (JUICE ONLY)

COCKTAILS OF THE
"GAY NINETIES"

The recipes in this group will be of particular interest to the younger set, who are eternally being reminded of the "good old days" before prohibition. With these they may draw their own conclusions as to the relative merits of the drinks of yesterday and today.

Father and grandfather, (not mother, she drank tea and lemonade) will still argue that "those were the days" of real drinking, and proper drinking, too. Dad will maintain, if given half a chance, that the gentleman of the waning years of the nineteenth century knew his liquor and how to take it—and when to stop. And he will tell you that the whiskies and brandies of then were better than can be had today.

Without attempting to take any sides in this matter it is interesting to note that the kinds of cocktails served in the "Gay Nineties" were definitely fewer in number. There were less than forty variations of the Great American Drink served commonly at that time. Of course many of the "stand-bys" of today were being mixed then, notably the Manhattan and the Old Fashioned, but the Martini of now seems to have originally been known as the Martinez. At least in the recipe lists of the old days there appears the Martinez, and it is described "same as Manhattan, substituting Gin for Whiskey".

(Continued From Opposite Page)

Such familiar acquaintances of these days as the Bronx, the Side
Car, the Orange Blossom, and the Stinger are not to be found in
the old books. On the other hand, we do come across many that
are definitely dated by their names, like the Trilby and the Buster
Brown, unheard of today.

Judging by the recipes in the old books, the changes made in
the concoction of cocktails of the same names today are not ex-
actly radical. In fact the differences are trifling in the main, still
we know that just a dash of this or that can mean a lot to the
palate.

At any rate, it was our thought that you might like to study these
cocktails of our fathers, these mixtures of the "Gay Nineties", so
here is a fairly complete list of them.

BLACKTHORNE

1/2 WINEGLASS SLOE GIN
1/2 WINEGLASS FRENCH VERMOUTH
1 TEASPOON SYRUP
2 DASHES LEMON JUICE
2 DASHES ORANGE BITTERS
1 DASH ANGOSTURA BITTERS

ABSINTHE

1 PONY ABSINTHE
1 WINEGLASS WATER
  (POUR IN SLOWLY)
1 TEASPOON SYRUP
2 DASHES ANGOSTURA BITTERS

GOLDEN BELL

1 JIGGER SHERRY
1 PONY VERMOUTH
3 DASHES ORANGE BITTERS
1 PIECE ORANGE PEEL

CHAMPAGNE

1 SMALL LUMP ICE
1 LUMP SUGAR
2 DASHES ANGOSTURA BITTERS
1 TWIST LEMON PEEL
CHAMPAGNE TO FILL GLASS

CLUB

3/4 JIGGER OLD BRANDY
2 DASHES MARASCHINO
2 DASHES PINEAPPLE JUICE
2 DASHES BITTERS
MIX WITH ICE AND STRAIN, DRESS
WITH STRAWBERRIES AND TWIST OF
LEMON PEEL, ADD DASH OF
CHAMPAGNE.

DERONDA

2/3 PLYMOUTH GIN
1/3 CALISAYA

EXPRESS

1 PONY SCOTCH
1 PONY ITALIAN VERMOUTH
2 DROPS SYRUP
3 DASHES ORANGE BITTERS

LONE TREE

1 WINEGLASS TOM GIN
1 PONY ITALIAN VERMOUTH

OLD SPORT

1/2 JIGGER RYE
1/2 JIGGER SHERRY
2 TEASPOONS SYRUP
1 TEASPOON PINEAPPLE SYRUP
2 DASHES ORANGE BITTERS
1 DASH PEYSCHAND'S BITTERS
RINSE COCKTAIL GLASS WITH
ABRICOTINE. STRAIN INTO SAME,
DASH WITH SELTZER AND DRESS
WITH FRUIT.

BUSTER BROWN

1 JIGGER WHISKEY
2 DASHES LEMON JUICE
1 TEASPOON SYRUP
2 DASHES ORANGE BITTERS

BRANDY

1 WINEGLASS FINE BRANDY
2 DASHES ANGOSTURA BITTERS
1 TEASPOON SYRUP
1 TWIST LEMON PEEL

COUNTRY

1 JIGGER RYE
2 DASHES ANGOSTURA BITTERS
2 DASHES ORANGE BITTERS
1 PIECE LEMON PEEL

GOLF LINKS

1/2 WINEGLASS RYE
1/2 WINEGLASS SWEET CATAWBA
2 DASHES LEMON JUICE
1 TEASPOON SYRUP
2 DASHES ORANGE BITTERS
1 DASH ANGOSTURA BITTERS
1 DASH RUM
RINSE COCKTAIL GLASS WITH
ABRICOTINE, STRAIN INTO SAME,
DASH WITH APOLLINARIS AND
DRESS WITH FRUIT.

GIN

1 WINEGLASS GIN
1 TEASPOON SYRUP
2 DASHES ORANGE BITTERS
1 DASH ANGOSTURA BITTERS
1 PIECE LEMON PEEL

DIXIE WHISKEY

1 JIGGER WHISKEY
1 LUMP SUGAR (DISSOLVED)
1 DASH LEMON JUICE
2 DASHES ANGOSTURA BITTERS
1 DASH CURACAO
5 DROPS CREME DE MENTHE

DUPLEX

1/2 ITALIAN VERMOUTH
1/2 FRENCH VERMOUTH
3 DASHES ORANGE BITTERS
3 DASHES ACID PHOSPHATE

FANCY BRANDY

1 JIGGER FINE BRANDY
1 DASH ORANGE BITTERS
2 DASHES ANGOSTURA BITTERS
3 DASHES MARASCHINO
MOISTEN RIM OF GLASS WITH
PIECE OF LEMON AND DIP IN
POWDERED SUGAR.

HARVARD

1 1/2 PONIES BRANDY
1 PONY ITALIAN VERMOUTH
3 DASHES ANGOSTURA BITTERS
1 DASH GUM SYRUP
STRAIN INTO A COCKTAIL GLASS,
FILL WITH SELTZER AND SERVE
QUICKLY.

MARTINEZ

1/2 GIN
1/2 ITALIAN VERMOUTH
1 DASH ANGOSTURA BITTERS
1/2 BARSPOON SUGAR
1 TWIST LEMON PEEL

MANHATTAN

1/2 WHISKEY
1/2 ITALIAN VERMOUTH
1 DASH ANGOSTURA BITTERS
1/2 BARSPOON SUGAR
1 TWIST LEMON PEEL

METROPOLE

3/4 JIGGER BRANDY
1/2 JIGGER FRENCH VERMOUTH
2 DASHES GUM SYRUP
1 DASH ORANGE BITTERS
2 DASHES ANGOSTURA BITTERS

OLD FASHIONED

1 LUMP SUGAR
1 DASH SELTZER
(CRUSH SUGAR WITH MUDDLER)
1 CUBE ICE
1 JIGGER WHISKEY
1 DASH ORANGE BITTERS
1 DASH ANGOSTURA BITTERS
1 PIECE LEMON PEEL
STIR GENTLY AND SERVE WITH
A SPOON.

OLD TOM GIN

1 WINEGLASS OLD TOM GIN
3 DASHES GUM SYRUP
2 DASHES ANGOSTURA BITTERS
2 DASHES CURACAO
1 TWISTED LEMON PEEL

SARATOGA

1 PONY BRANDY
1 PONY WHISKEY
1 PONY VERMOUTH
1 SLICE LEMON

TRILBY

2/3 WHISKEY
1/3 CALISAYA
3 DASHES ORANGE BITTERS
3 DASHES ACID PHOSPHATE

IRISH

1 WINEGLASS IRISH WHISKEY
1 PONY ITALIAN VERMOUTH
3 DASHES ORANGE BITTERS
2 DASHES ACID PHOSPHATE

TUXEDO

3/4 JIGGER TOM GIN
1/2 JIGGER ITALIAN VERMOUTH
1 BARSPOON SHERRY WINE
1 DASH ANGOSTURA BITTERS

WHISKEY

1 JIGGER WHISKEY
1 LUMP SUGAR (DISSOLVED)
1 DASH LEMON JUICE
2 DASHES ANGOSTURA BITTERS

WHISKEY (NEW YORK)

1 JIGGER WHISKEY
1/2 JIGGER ITALIAN VERMOUTH
1/2 TEASPOON SHERRY WINE
2 DASHES ANGOSTURA BITTERS
1 TWIST LEMON PEEL

VERMOUTH

1 1/2 PONIES FRENCH VERMOUTH
3 DASHES ANGOSTURA BITTERS
2 DASHES GUM SYRUP

STAR

3/4 JIGGER APPLE BRANDY
1/2 JIGGER ITALIAN VERMOUTH
2 DASHES GUM SYRUP
3 DASHES ORANGE BITTERS
1 TWIST LEMON PEEL

RISING SUN

1 WINEGLASS BRANDY
1 TEASPOON CURACAO
1 TEASPOON PINEAPPLE SYRUP
3 DASHES ANGOSTURA BITTERS
2 DASHES MARASCHINO
1 TWIST LEMON PEEL

REMEMBER—
THESE COCKTAILS WERE THE VOGUE LONG BEFORE PROHIBITION, SO
WHEN A RECIPE CALLS FOR A JIGGER IT MEANS TWO FULL OUNCES.

"LET ME PLAY THE FOOL, WITH MIRTH AND LAUGHTER LET OLD
WRINKLES COME; AND LET MY LIVER RATHER HEAT WITH WINE,
THAN MY HEART COOL WITH MORTIFYING GROANS."
- SHAKESPEARE

INDEX

Index to
Cocktails of the "Gay Nineties"

GLASSWARE CHART

A GUIDE TO THE PROPER USE OF THE VARIOUS DESIGNS IN GLASSWARE

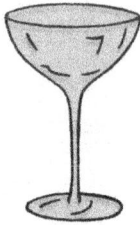
Hollow Stem Champagne

Standard Wine

Secondary Wine

Rhine Wine

Great Burghundy

Creme de Menthe

Champagne

Small Cocktail

Large Cocktail

Champagne Flute

Sherry

Cordials

Pousse-Cafe

Port Wine

Liqueur

Brandy

Old-Fashioned

Highball

Brandy + Soda

Whiskey

MIXED DRINKS

A BARTENDER'S GUIDE

Compiled and Edited by

W. C. WHITFIELD
DECORATED BY TAD SHELL

Available at

WWW.ENGAGEBOOKS.CA

www.ingramcontent.com/pod-product-compliance
Lightning Source LLC
Chambersburg PA
CBHW031615040426
42452CB00006B/526